Dark Harvest

New & Selected Poems, 2001–2020

Books by Joseph Millar

Overtime
Fortune
Blue Rust
Kingdom

Dark Harvest

New & Selected Poems, 2001–2020

Joseph Millar

Carnegie Mellon University Press
Pittsburgh 2021

Acknowledgments

Thanks to the editors of the following journals, where these poems first appeared:

Academy of American Poets: Poem-a-Day: "Venetian Siesta"
Alaska Quarterly Review: "Forgiveness," "Meadow"
Catamaran: "Mistletoe"
Limp Wrist: "Epithalamion"
Northwest Review: "Venriloquist"
Orion: "Corvus"
Prairie Schooner: "Pablo and Me," "Memorial Day Meditation"
Willow Springs: "Affluence"

Special thanks also to Michael McGriff who put this selection together, Gerald Costanzo, Marvin Bell, Dorianne Laux, Cynthia Lamb, Connie Amoroso, Matthew Dickman, Sharon Olds, Tyree Daye, Kwame Dawes, Arielle Hebert, Wilton Barnhardt, Matt Wimberly, Pacific University MFA, North Carolina State MFA, Virginia Center for the Creative Arts, John-Roger and John Morton.

Book design by Martina Rethman

Library of Congress Control Number 2021937532
ISBN 978-0-88748-672-2

10 9 8 7 6 5 4 3 2

for Charles Rosier Millar (1946-2019)

There are no roads but the frost.

—James Wright

Contents

from Overtime (2001)

from Fortune (2007)

New Poems

from Overtime (2001)

Telephone Repairman

All morning in the February light
he has been mending cable,
splicing the pairs of wires together
according to their colors,
white-blue to white-blue
violet-slate to violet-slate,
in the warehouse attic by the river.

When he is finished
the messages will flow along the line:
thank you for the gift,
please come to the baptism,
the bill is now past due:
voices that flicker and gleam back and forth
across the tracer-colored wires.

We live so much of our lives
without telling anyone,
going out before dawn,
working all day by ourselves,
shaking our heads in silence
at the news on the radio.
He thinks of the many signals
flying in the air around him,
the syllables fluttering,
saying *please love me*
from continent to continent
over the curve of the earth.

Names I'd Forgotten

I used to get drunk in the morning, starting awake
in the sinister warmth of the couch, tangled up
in my raincoat and pants like a trapped animal.
I'd follow the rusted-out tracks to the store,
ignoring the alien mothers with laundry, the crows
on the trash bin, the cryptic remarks
of the grocer looking out at the rain
and asking when it would stop,
smiling as he slid the fifth into its narrow bag
like a man loading artillery. The day would flare briefly
and disappear, its singed dust prickling my scalp.
I'd listen to gravel trucks snarl in the alley, the crows
with their bandaged voices, my oldest child
calling my name from the shadows
3,000 miles away. And study
the streetlight's fractured reflections
like stars whose names I'd forgotten.

Fiber Optics

On Labor Day the last barbecue smoke
        had drifted into the branches
and Public TV showed the legendary strike
          at J&L Steel in Aliquippa,
the cops opening fire
    on the workers' picnic, the men in shirtsleeves running,
the women, some carrying children, falling in the Pennsylvania dirt.
I'm thinking about this,
    driving my new truck down Highway 280,
getting twelve miles to the gallon on the company credit card
        with a storm coming in from the west.

We're working nights and weekends pulling wire
    into the ceilings of Silicon Valley,
moving our ladders just ahead of the drywall crews
    with their knives of adhesive,
        their radios blasting Metallica,
the carpet gang in the finished wing
        spreading beige-colored glue on the floor,
nobody talking, hurrying along in the midnight glare of the heat lamps.

Impossible anyone here would strike,
    though we're comrades of sorts
        and hungry for something,
listening to rain pound the glass doors
    of this palace paid for by venture capitalists
whose appetite nobody questions.

    Inside it's a hardware bonanza: boxes
of galvanized fasteners overflow onto the Visqueen tarp
        that covers the stairs like a membrane.
Somebody squats by the telephone switch
wiring Teflon patch bays into steel racks
    and testing each pathway
        the delicate voltages follow.

Everybody wants to work, the more hours the better,
especially the young ones, snowy with gypsum dust, wolfing their lunch
        on a stack of new two-by-fours
while the overtime keeps piling up
                        like valet parking behind the first tee
where the developers and union reps, weekday afternoons
                gather to discuss trade.

Outside the trenches and conduits slowly fill with water
and two of us crouch in a low cement box,
                        adjusting the filament cable,
the fiberglass link that feeds the big hubs.
And nobody's wondering about Karl Marx or the poems of Cesare Pavese.

We're trying to stay down out of the wind
and close up the resin-filled splice case
        so the ghostlight signal can travel across,
sending its neuron-flickering code
                        as fast as a man can think.

Spanish Blues

I want to cry saying my name
rose, child and fir on the shore of this lake . . .
—Frederico García Lorca, "Double Poem of Lake Eden"

Late afternoon in the Hayward marsh
I had no desire to speak my name
as I sat in my patched raingear
reading about the life of Lorca.
Not to the gravel thrown up on the banks
or the egret feathers and guano
and not to the fox who came out of the reeds,
red fur streaked with tidewater,
who glanced at me sideways and vanished
in the rough grass of the estuary.

Watching its small tracks fill in the dim light
I felt my body settle deeper,
remembering things I'd stolen—
flowers, the red tool box—
and never told anyone;
kindnesses and love betrayed,
nights of false promise whispered
into the ears of believing women,
their children eyeing the door while I packed.

There was no gypsy music like his
rising from the hills of my childhood—
no tree of song branching up from the earth
with guitars that hovered like birds of prey.
And I was no solitary horseman
with olives in my saddlebags
kicking up dust on the narrow road.

But as I squatted in the salt marsh,
the lights of a tanker winking on near the bridge,
I felt this desire to sing about death
and to praise the deep pools and shoreline

of the fallen landscape that held me.
Three days past the end of my fiftieth year
the tide lay slack on the Hayward flats,
its husks of dead starfish trapped in the mud
and the sky turning dark as the sea.

Outside Monterey

Outside Monterey the highway
runs by the sea and the torch singer
on the radio has a voice like twilight:
"I couldn't love you more, child,
if time was running out . . ."

My ten-year-old shaved his head when his mother left,
looked oddly more adult last night,
coloring the Stay Out sign for his bedroom door.
Earlier I stopped to buy goldfish, dinner
for the snake he keeps trapped with its hunger
in a glass box.

Night drifts into the artichoke fields
and the swallows veer off toward the hills,
bent wings scissoring the dusk.
I park under a tree, lean back
with the lights off and the engine running.

I want to travel all night like this,
the ocean whispering beside me in the darkness,
passing no one on the road.

Midlife

She's slim and seems distracted, the social worker
who visits my apartment, who wants to know
why my ten-year-old was alone New Year's Eve
when the cops came through the door.

His mother was drunk, I say, and I was up north
with my girlfriend who doesn't want any more kids.
Would she like a cup of tea?
We do have some problems here, I know—
as I force-feed old newspapers into the trash—
but hopefully nothing too unseemly,
no disarray that can't be explained.

I want to say I've tried
to find another way to live,
away from the electric metal wires
that whisper to me in the afternoons,
the snake dreams that follow after,
uncoiling slowly in my sleep
and the supermarkets where I go unconscious,
humming to myself and staring, minutes at a time,
at the olives and loaves of bread.

There's not much to show for all this:
four rooms, a dented Olds, tattered pictures
of Che Guevara and Muhammad Ali,
the Sixties with their fire and music
scattered like highway cinders. Does the State
offer therapy for aging single fathers?
Is it all right to smoke?
Would she like to step into the back where it's dark
and fuck, standing up amid the laundry?
She smiles vaguely, hands me her card,
says she won't need to return.

Later I think this must be what it is
to get older. My knee hurts getting up

from the couch. Can't work like I used to
and my chest hairs are turning gray.
I'm angry with my son, now quietly asleep
for needing help with everything: homework,
breakfast, rinsing the shampoo from his hair;
and sad, as I gather his small raincoat,
the baseball hat saying Surf's Up,
hang them over a chair, and start washing the pot
of day-old spaghetti we ate for dinner.

I listen to Miles with the lights off,
knowing the phone won't ring any more
and too tired to shower. I listen to my breath
leave and return, rain falling
into the cold trackless night
and the wind in the trees outside
like someone passing.

Selling Out at the Top of the World

for John

Nobody spoke in the Arctic cold those mornings we rode
over wrecked lunar fields following tracks to the dynamite shed.
       Not the drillers from Oklahoma in ski masks
and insulated coveralls, not the Eskimos from Barrow,
some wearing only down vests and flannel; not even us,
       the survey helpers, tears and snot
           from the freezing wind lacing our faces in ice.

We'd screw the cans of explosive together, load the steel chain
and transit and start driving north to the line
       where leads of dark seawater
flexed through the ice like a wound that refused to heal.
Scrabbling across sloped pressure ridges and planting
       wire flags in the crust,
we knew our charts would someday be sold to Nixon's cohorts,
Exxon and Richfield, that the Revolution had come north
       to freeze under the waters of Prudhoe Bay.

       Scattered across the north slope
of the Brooks Range, countless gypsy seismograph crews
       scratched and gouged in twilit shadows,
prospecting the ocean floor. The ice where we lived grew
six feet thick over the Beaufort Sea, and we clustered like flies
       at the top of the world, watching the sun
creep like a slow fuse partway around the horizon,
soft light shining back from the surface, hanging the air with ghosts:
       mountains upside down
at our feet, white buildings hovering half out of the sea,
and the moon on its back, refusing to set
       over the ragged plains.

If our hearts had been pure we'd have grieved
       for ourselves or found other wages farther south.
Instead we surrendered to spasms of laughter in the anaesthetic cold,
       making up names for the Texas bosses:

Black Jack, Sidewinder, Big Tomato; planning the movie
we'd someday write, a noir-Western starring Richard Widmark's
        pale narrow eyes and rictus grin.

Wyatt Earp and Jim Bowie had nothing down on our Okie drillers,
        who'd flown here from the Middle East
    with stories we listened to evenings, of jeweled
            Arabian sunsets or the withering
sandstorms of Egypt, where Muslim laborers
        were called back to work from their prayers
            by numbers they wore on their backs.

Here we only stopped work to wolf candy bars
        or piss in the frozen tracks of the boom truck.
Nobody wanted to say much about home, though one spoke
of the Sacramento delta where he'd worked as a brakeman
        for Southern Pacific, gone to high school
with the Mitchell brothers before they became pornography kings.

Some were here to escape other lives, ex-wives and children,
        jail time down south,
many just back from Vietnam. Who knew if they'd watched the live
demonstrations where people like us dodged tear gas, the walls
        of our communal houses on fire
with Che Guevara's austere face or the thunderbird of Cesar Chavez?
        Here the Indians never looked straight
        at anyone white
and the stiff wings of winter
    closed down on us all, as though
    we'd been born without histories
        to this godless landscape of ice and bent light.

When we got loose in town we paid whores from L.A.
a hundred extra to dine with us in the Gold Rush Room of the Anchorage Westin.
I fell quickly in love with mine, her black nails sparkling
        like onyx rain
as she turned her wrist to look at her watch.

They harvested our amnesiac wages the way pipeliners
        empty an oil field.
No one could wait to sell out for a fortune, be rid of the Sixties
experiments—ecology, brotherhood, socialism—except maybe
        the cook from Baton Rouge
who'd lost fifteen grand playing dice at the Embers
and wanted us to help get it back.

        Not much would ever be given back
to the wilderness beginning to crack and thaw over the bright seams
of moonlight near the drilling rigs on the sea. Not the underground
        swamp gas rising through cleavages
forced apart by the drills, not the patches of tundra scarred
by surveyors trying to leave tracks in the storm,
        not even the ridges of this winter's ice
          glowing like quartz in the tractor lamps.

When we returned camp was moving again, exhaust fumes
hanging the air like a shroud, two D-8 Cats towing trailers on sleds
    over ashen terrain toward Canada.
We watched from above in the company chopper, hovering over
the dim caravan, eating chocolate and taking quick swigs of scotch,
    the smell of death frozen into the night,
fuel oil, diesel smoke, leaf-mold pre-dating
the kingdom of Solomon, the collapsed insides of the dinosaur,
    the decomposed skull of the mastodon
turning the cold steel rotors of time
        under the blind April stars.

Sole Custody

Today he'll ride his bike to Safeway
in his death's head earring and mismatched socks,
where the checkers all know his name. He'll buy
Cheetos and Kool-Aid before coming home to bathe
in the rusty light from the TV, until I get off work
and collapse on the fake velvet sofa, a double order
of fast food bleeding grease through a bag in my fist.
He hasn't eaten anything green in a week
and I see the dirt under his fingernail when he points
to the surfboard he drew on his sneaker.

What would we do if I got fired, I wonder,
listening to the wind and the evening's lead story
announcing more layoffs in the South Bay. There's enough
in the bank for his school clothes, and the rent's
almost paid again. I should be happier.
He's been watching the talk shows. Have
you ever done it with someone you didn't love,
he asks, his old guitar resting against the wall
like an abandoned girlfriend, and the pleats
of the houndstooth flea market slacks
gathered around his small waist
like the leaves of a sunflower calyx.
Eat slowly, I say, as he smiles at me
around a mouthful of fries, points the clicker
at my chest and says I'm getting fat.

We're bound together like sailors, swaying across
a dark ocean, resigned to each other's odd humors
and unable to see the stars overhead
as we stagger around in the engine room
of a ship with a foreign name.

Heart Attack

You've always suspected the voice of defiance
would carry you only so far, wondering
when your life might end
even as you lounged on the high school steps
smoking a Lucky Strike.
In those days you considered it honorable
to make yourself drunk with fear,
climbing the abandoned cement plant's silos
or driving flat out with no headlights over the river road,
while Buddy Holly's "That'll Be the Day"
spilled all summer from dashboard speakers
in the slow fat days before Vietnam.

And you never outgrew the thrill of resistance,
the reckless desire to be stricken with dread.
In the Halloween parade years later,
wired on amphetamines and port wine,
you became afraid to look off to your left—
where the scarlet candles and black paper skulls
fluttered and spun through the wind—
toward the spot where Castaneda says
the angel of death walks beside you,
trailing one wing like a bandage
into the autumn smoke.

Now you're listening to a ragged cough
on the far side of the curtain, your neighbor
cursing in tremulous Spanish, his moan
like the dirge of some Catholic ghost.
You're trying to make a deal with God,
whispering an embarrassed farewell
to red meat and cigarettes,
to your insolence and pitiable hauteur.
You're wired to a twelve-volt electrical harness
under a stiffening veil of dried sweat, your chest
a patchwork of shaved gray stubble,
rib cage plastered with ultrasound gel.

You're not seeing much in the way of a vision
unless it's the fractured sand-colored light
stuttering from your hospital TV

where a lone outlaw rides for the Texas border.
The posse's closed off the canyon behind him
and the sunlight's falling in clots through the trees.
He's splashing his horse downriver,
trying to cover his trail.

My Father and Thomas Wyatt in Hefka's Bar

He was awful to service people when he was drinking,
this renegade literary child of the rich,
his family inheritance long since spent,
announcing his exile from the common man
in a strange quaint language, silvered with alcohol,
calling the waitress "Charming lass"
like some toss-pot Elizabethan.
I'd be ashamed to look at the woman,
silently wishing I'd never come home,
that I'd stayed where I was, milking the overtime
painting houses or shoveling fish.
Sometimes it was dangerous, like the night
he was waving a tennis racket by the jukebox
in Kelleher's Roadhouse. They were ready to kill him
in his seersucker jacket, his knit tie askew at his chin
and I still don't know how we made it to the car.

One Christmas I found him pounding the bar at Hefka's
with three unemployed miners muttering ominously
in the bruised light by the shuffleboard game.
The frayed elk was glaring down through the smoke,
nostrils flared in warning, antlers glazed
with nicotine and shellac. I perched beside him
on a torn red stool by the jars of hardboiled eggs,
the slow fan prickling my scalp.

But that night was different. The talk
at the bar flowed on as before
and the shuffleboard players turned away
as the tables began to come alive with the day shift
from Bethlehem Steel. By midnight Johnny Cash
was rumbling sorrowfully into the haze,
I'd won three beers playing darts, and my father
was quoting Wyatt, his voice drifting easily
over the iambs and into the chapped face
of a teamster from Elders Ridge.

Maybe they let it pass that time
because they could tell we were father and son
and the backlit Santa by the phone booth
smoking a fake Dutch Masters cheroot
protected us as we stumbled with our six-packs
over the frozen mud to the car.
It had started to snow and my father was singing
"Heart of My Heart" in the front seat,
jubilant and half-redeemed by this company
of working men, by the free one
the Polish bartender slid toward us just before closing.

Poem for a New Girlfriend

I'm driving down the highway in the dark
on my way to pick you up
with the ocean on one side
and raindrops spattering the windshield,
balancing a Coke between my legs.
If a baby were asleep in the front seat,
nothing would wake it,
not the hiss of the long grass
waving by the sea wall,
not the cypress branches groaning in the wind
or the dim necklaces of surf
tumbling onto the sand.

I'm afraid to do anything sudden
on this wet pavement,
afraid to change direction or speed up,
to give you the small bracelet
I bought today in the Castro
or to say anything about the future,
as though the car might slide sideways
or the doors fly open.
So the baby would go on sleeping,
a pale shadow beside me,
stirring slightly perhaps, its hands
like stars in the glow from the dash.

Impossible to tell
what snowlit oceans
might be swaying under its eyelids,
with no cars on the road
and the lights out front
all turning green in the rain.

Hansel and Gretel's Father

On days when the small boy now asleep
asks me for money and movie tickets
I can't see any escape. I want to banish
playgrounds, the circus, and all bright colors
and I don't want to hear anyone laugh.
If I don't get this electric bill paid
something bad will happen.

Bottlecaps, water guns and X-Men cards
are scattered all over the homemade fort
in the garage. A Fred Flintstone mask
hangs from my truck antenna
and it's almost time for me to go to work.
I'm yelling at him
in front of his wide-eyed friends
and he sobs, sitting on his bicycle
with his hat on backwards.

He may never understand this fierce satisfaction,
watching him eat vegetables at supper,
as though the green stalk fibers and the juice
were entering my own body.
Have some more, I mutter,
the shadow behind me pressing me down
into my own dark footprints.

I don't think the woodcutter wanted gold
or even the manic afternoon sex
his witch of a wife might have promised
if he would only get rid of the kids. Probably
he just wanted to make enough
to feed everybody.

Dark Harvest

for Annie

You can come to me in the evening,
      with the fingers of former lovers
fastened in your hair and their ghost lips
      opening over your body.
They can be philosophers or musicians in long coats and colored shoes
and they can be smarter than I am,
      whispering to each other
          when they look at us.

You can come walking toward my window after dusk
      when I can't see past the lamplight in the glass,
when the chipped plates rattle on the counter
      and the cinders dance on the crossties
      under the wheels of southbound freights.

Bring children if you want, and the long wounds of sisters
      branching away
          behind you toward the sea.
Bring your mother's tense distracted face
      and the shoulders of plane mechanics
slumped in the Naugahyde booths of the airport diner
      waiting for you to bring their eggs.

I'll bring all the bottles of gin I drank by myself
      and my cracked mouth opened partway
as I slept in the back of my blue Impala
          dreaming of spiders.

I won't forget the lines running deep
      in the cheeks of the Polish landlady
who wouldn't let the cops upstairs,
      the missing ring finger of the machinist from Spenard
whose money I stole after he passed out to go downtown in a cab
and look for whores,
      or the trembling lower jaw of my son, watching me

back my motorcycle from his mother's driveway one last time,
      the ribbons and cone-shaped birthday hats
scattered on the lawn,
         the rain coming down like broken glass.

We'll go out under the stars and sit together on the ground
      and there will be enough to eat for everybody.
They can sleep on my couches and rug
         and the next day
I'll go to work, stepping easily across the scaffolding, feeding
the cable gently into the new pipes on the roof
        and dreaming
like St. Francis of the still dark rocks
that disappear under the morning tide,
      only to climb back into the light,
sea-rimed, salt-blotched, their patched webs of algae
blazing with flies in the sun.

Love Pirates

I follow with my mouth the small wing of muscle
under your shoulder, lean over your back, breathing
into your hair and thinking of nothing. I want
to lie down with you under the sails of a wooden sloop
and drift away from all of it, our two cars rusting
in the parking lot, our families whining like tame geese
at feeding time, and all the bosses of the earth
cursing the traffic in the morning haze.

They will telephone each other from their sofas
and glass desks, with no idea where we could be,
unable to picture the dark throat
of the saxophone playing upriver, or the fire
we gather between us on this fantail of dusty light,
having stolen a truckload of roses
and thrown them into the sea.

Waking Up After Reading Proust

Maybe the heart decides while we sleep
what to remember
and the lights of a coal truck
sweeping our walls at midnight
will revisit us as an angel's face
we have already known.

Last week my son trod the dusty stage
of the living room carpet, secretly proud
in Egyptian dress, an elfin scribe to the Pharoah,
his mother's bracelets jangling
on thin forearms as he held up the reed pen
fashioned from wire and thread, the hieroglyphs for "water,"
and the map copied out on shirt cardboard
to describe the Nile at flood.

I wondered if April's hennaed dusk
would leave its stain in his memory
as he reckoned the scribe's tasks on pale fingers:
keeping track of taxes and marriages, births, deaths
and bushels of wheat—charting the arable land
of the kingdom, mapping the boundaries that disappeared
under the river each spring.

Everything I wanted then was close at hand:
the juice glass glowing like a lamp behind him,
the smell of onions deepening over the stove,
dark violin phrases twisting
from the radio into the air.
I remembered the resinous shadows
under the lid of the cedar chest
where my grandmother kept the toys:
the cowboy hat, the wooden sword, the chipped
hull of the plaster sailboat; and the winter light
ebbing away through the elms on Montgomery Avenue.

And maybe the brown pond gleaming
like an amniotic veil
under the arbor at Swann's estate
leads down to that darker ocean Jung says belongs
to everyone. Over the deep-sea fracture zones
where the gods jostle and shove,
its tides keep bearing the fragments up
into more peaceful water:

hawthorn cluster and village steeple,
the madeleine soaked in lime-blossom tea,
all shining with mud and phosphorus
on the dream's brief shoreline
before the waves close over us again.

from Fortune (2007)

Feeding Tristem's Snake

Light brings out nubs in the black felt rug
spattered with chalky waste like a bird's
which the rat is trying to scurry beneath
having sensed something wrong in the stillness.
This rat I've hand-fed popcorn and raspberries,
pink feet and round hairless tail
translucent, shivering beneath the glass.

I hover above, pale version of Shiva
who yesterday smote the arched vault
of the termite, hacked open
the ant's teeming galleries, tore out
webbed roots of kudzu and columbine,
put the torch to the wasp's paper cells—
entranced by the row of dark
emblems flowering down the scaled back,
the bone seam dividing her sloped
naked face as the jaws unhinge
and the great throat surges.

Hansel and Gretel's Father Explains

Children, I chose the woman
because her skirts rustled
when she undressed and because
she'd bring my lunch to the woods
and sit close on a fallen log, one hand
on my leg, watching me eat.
In winter the flowers her body
smelled of helped me forget the wind
sharpening itself like an axe blade
over the frozen lake. God help me,
I wanted to sleep forever
curled up at her narrow breast.
How many times I've followed the path
we took that last day through the trees,
the ravens' iron voices mocking
my flesh. I dreamed I saw
a boy's blond hair matted with blood,
the burned face of a woman seven feet tall,
my crimes the damp sperm blossoms
under her dress. And maybe I've only
dreamed this: spring rain in the forest,
new grass in the fields, your hands
holding mine in the uneasy clasp,
restless, hesitant, partially feigned,
of childhood's helpless forgiveness.

Junkyard

Except for the goldenrod covered with dust
and the blue cinders under the tracks,
except for the gondolas loaded with scrap iron
like boxes of flowers unpacked by the dead,
this could be a church for the resurrection
of car thieves past and still serving time.

Gear oil and antifreeze leech into the ground.
I can see distant tidal basins glowing
like mercury off to the west. Who will be left
to pardon us now, the boy with crosses
tattooed on both hands who rolled
the stripped Thunderbird into the river?

Or the machinist laid off from Bethlehem Steel—
axle grease anointing each knuckle—
who hot-wired a Chrysler parked by the gates,
its cylinders firing, fan blades spinning
free in their rusty shroud, the stopped world
looking up, amazed, stuck like a boot in its own black mud.

Environmentalist

Mars's scarred face hangs like a blind clock
over the road, its closest orbit
in thousands of years, shedding its purple light
on thistles and sun-blasted dandelions.
The twin fires burning outside Bend
keep drawing closer together.
We're a hundred miles west
near Monroe, the evening air adrift
like a shroud, red pollen billowing
down from the elms. I've squeezed
past wrecked washing machines
and a rusted-out engine hung from a chain
knocked on the patched Airstream's door,
to ask the tall man in suspenders
for five bucks to help clean up the river.

I can't tell if he's laughing or crying,
his eye sockets dark craters broken
into his brow's tattered ridge.
His small dog growls, snaps at my shoes.
Behind him the news channel
stutters and leaps. Pale stubble covers
his fissured cheeks, a big vein
in his temple. He says the mill
closed twelve years ago, waves me away
like a fly, his right hand missing two fingers.

Mystery Tramp

In the steady stare of a homeless man,
his newspaper rolled up like a club, my father
eyes me without rage or grief, smelling
of port wine and death. He peers out
from the wings of his overcoat,
the downtown library behind him
smoldering with language, music and poetry,
numbers, prophecy, science. His voice
is a whisper as he thrusts a fingerless
glove palm-up in front of my face.
Maybe he'd like to stab me right here
next to the Civic Center, blue exhaust
from the Five McCallister drifting like ether
around us. *Where are you going and*
where have you been, he sang to the hills
on his last day alive, sipping whiskey
and milk on the porch, his Freud and Cervantes
stashed in their stale glue bindings.

He always thought death owed him extra
for the young wife he lost one piece
at a time, extra for the sons
who hid from his rages,
throwing rocks at the neighbor's windows
and flattening their frostbitten tulips
under a plywood sled. Too much
moonlight kept splashing down
on the house we would never own,
its driveway plowed under in springtime,
shallow footprints leading away into our
separate amnesias. Some of us would wander
for years from the docks to the Greyhound station
while sleet fell into the ravaged garden.
Sometimes I hear him groan just at nightfall,
a gray dove brooding above a small fire,
Queen Anne's lace like patches of spawn
spread over the frozen hillsides.

Middle Age

Narrowing pond fringed with algae.
Ivy trailing its bracelets and lutes,
wrinkled sunlight of autumn.
We like the bottomlands, easing
a friend's car past muddy sloughs
chocked with lilies and watercress,
tan Mississippi spreading its banks
into islands and fan-shaped deltas.
Here's where the Vietnamese immigrants
hunt for catfish and squirrels,
casting off in their four-foot skiffs
ten thousand miles from the place
they were born and never getting lost.

Tools

I was sixty days without a drink
working the back of the Howard Street store,
cleaning the tools my boss scavenged from basements
of tradesmen's widows all over the state.

I'd sort through the wrenches, boxes, and crescents
from Stanley, Craftsman, and Utica Tool,
bright sockets from Snap-on
we could charge twice as much for.
I'd polish the wrecking bars with WD-40,
the claw hammers, jack planes and pliers,
then clean up the handsaws, Henry Disston
and the best, London Springs,
twisting the studs from the filigreed handle
and sanding away the resinous shell
one stroke at a time
from the wide steel blade.

I seldom looked out through the dusty panes
at the rubble of Howard Street's
plywood-scabbed storefronts. I stayed
in the back near the cracked tubs of solvent
whose gray vapors ghosted the air—
and kept my eyes lowered, watching
the grinding wheel whirr in its armature,
cutting blue rust from the chisels and knives,
washing my knuckles in sparks.

Harriet Matthias Wickersham

They put me in charge of the big house
after the strokes finally took you,
left me alone in your sumptuous apartment
marking time till the final sale closed, watching
reruns of *The Untouchables* and smoking Panama red.
The furniture skulked in the corners
fuming with resin and must:
the mahogany armoire, the chest of drawers
stout relatives I'd met once as a child
carried away piece by piece
to their split-level in Cherry Hill.
My mother's portrait gleamed there, bright ghost
presiding over the wine-colored rug
where dense ethers rose from the garden.

I moved my friends in with their saxophones,
tapes of Bo Diddley and Howlin' Wolf.
Mr. Adler practiced Chopin upstairs
on a small baby grand. I collected
the rents. When the hot water
thermostat failed to shut off
steam rose from the sinks and toilets
till the supply pipe blew free of the heater
filling the basement with dark sludge.
Water surrounded us all that year:
The morning I thought I'd seen your face
in the lilac tree under the fire escape
I emptied your ashes into Westtown Lake
where my mother's had floated so long before.

I harried my pinched and narrow poems,
failed imitations of Tu Fu and James Wright.
Weekends I soaked through a languorous narcissism
in the opulent, claw-footed tub
under clouds of vapor, touching myself.
All I had was my body
which kept waking me up to eat, to shit,

to labor, hungover, for a local builder
at a piss-elegant site called Joie de Vivre,
fake mansions perched on a hillside
tricked out with gables and vaulted ceilings
in a sparse woods beside the Expressway.
I wore a red sweatshirt in winter,
burned trash in the bonfire, stacked scaffolding,
swung a pick into the frozen mud.

The night your lawyers signed salvage contracts
I stole the leaded smoke-blue windows,
the oak front door and its iron hasp,
tore out the off-white Williamsburg fireplace
while a fat moon lit the front porch like a pond
and a cold wind rattled the glistening bandage
of stapled plastic. I stashed
the goods in a storage locker,
thinking of my future fantasy home, then
never went back to claim them.

Grandmother, fragile, querulous solitary,
no one could stand you for long.
Your husband whose name you forbade us to speak
left the same year my mother was born,
driven out by your fits of pique.
And I was no prize myself
in my watch cap and worn Levi's
restless for California.

Lord knows I've never wished you'd come back,
though maybe you have, in another body,
one that's forgotten the evenings we enjoyed
in front of your television
Tuesday nights watching *Gunsmoke*
that rainy autumn I slept on the third floor—
you in the high bed drinking tea,
your aquiline head in a satin scarf

and I in the gold chair wrecked on hashish,
while fall storms blew through the sycamores
and the stern marshal kept order in Dodge.

Fall Night

Alone with Rilke's ghost in my taxi
parked somewhere near the Avenues

summer over, radio silent
waiting for the bars to close—

reading the one about autumn:
that he who's alone now will stay alone

write long letters and walk in the streets,
gray vagrant streets, ashen with moonlight

not knowing, not telling, no buses, no cars.
Dry leaves in the wind, Rilke's ghost

whispering to me under the dome light
that nothing I've seen will be forgotten:

not the marriages fallen apart or the son
grown to manhood without me,

not the money lost or the hours spent
wandering the amnesiac sand,

not the fire on the beach near the limestone flats
we never came back to, burned down to embers

or the twilight spreading its silent blue dust
over thirty bald eagles perched in the trees

gorging on thousands of infected carp
glittering in the shallows.

Red Wing

Here's where they make the good work shoes
in the long brick buildings beside the road.
Shoes whose stitched, crepe-wedge soles
and full-grain, oil-resistant leathers
bless tiny bones in the ankles and feet, shoes
of carpenters balanced on roof beams,
electricians, farmers, iron workers, welders—
cuffs frayed with sparks from the torch.
At shift's end the socks emerge tinged
pale orange, tops of the arches crisscrossed
with lace marks, propped up in front
of the six o'clock news. Here's to the sweet
breath of pond mist filling the lungs of summer.
Here's to baked beans and twelve hours off.
Here's to dust from the trucker's shoe, dust
he stepped into three states back.
Here's to shingles, aluminum flashing,
wall studs, rafters, ten-penny nails,
here's to tomatoes, onions and corn,
here's squatting down and here's reaching over,
here's to the ones who showed up.

Caroling

We clutched the purple mimeos
of "Joy to the World" and "God Rest Ye Merry"
as we sang a cappella, a bit out of time,
next to the fly-speckled angel
in the La Honda Home for the Aged.

The patients sat up straight in their pj's
under the fragrant pine boughs,
wheezed, giggled, clapped and waved.
And my brother walked out among them
bending down in his white shirt
to listen, nodding, giving away
the tissue-wrapped navel oranges.
Later he'd lead me to two old men
lying in neighboring beds, rough
faces deepened by weather,
big hands fleshy and scarred.
Clarence and Dale from North Dakota,
brothers who'd followed the wheat harvest,
picked apples together in Washington State.
Sometimes they need extra oxygen
and both of them suffer bad knees and feet
smiling broadly, without many teeth
after ninety-one Christmases.

Don't ask me why I've waited here
locked up inside the hours and years
or why I keep turning away.
Don't ask me why I wake up so early
and stand on the bridge before work
watching red leaves drift into the river
and thinking nothing will last.

Fortune

for my brothers

Because the long waves keep tearing gouges
into the curved banks of oyster shells,
because the dunes rose each evening
sudden and pale through the pines

because it was hard to see anything
the moon like a swan boat disappearing
into the deepening swell,

we listened
for our lost mother's voice
like one far out from land

the arms that held us
the cloud of dark hair,

because we couldn't remember her face
we hid out with our Cokes and stolen Pall Malls,
our jackknives and Three Musketeers bars

where the willows hung down their branches
over the knotted grass,
where the granite rose up behind us
leaning out toward the stars.

We were striped mackerel holding still
three fathoms down
up to our eyes in darkness

while the surf raged over Halibut Point
and the channel bell rocked in the tide.

What is time to one playing a song
through the teeth of a broken comb?

How could we know the shapes of men
hidden inside us, angular, clenched,
or the women waiting far up ahead
rich in their membranes of milk and blood

as we crouched above the scorched campfire stones
carrying the seeds of our kind.

Potter's Field

The detective in charge, slender, bored,
dusts sandwich crumbs from his vest,
recites the service bestowed on each corpse:
inked fingerprints, a photograph,
then a clean pine box whose resinous planks
hold off most blight and fungus, at least
for the blink of an eye. They pile up the coffins
twelve deep, not twenty feet from the estuary
and prisoners backfill the trench by hand,
turning away from the smell.

Some say the earth belongs to the dead,
even those with no name
and no metal angel's rusted bare feet
sunk in the mud. My grandfather
could be buried here, the one nobody
will tell me about. Sometimes I'm grateful
he left no memories, it's enough
that his chapped drifter's eyelids
under my hat brim keep stinging now
as the moon backs away
from the marshland's incoming tide.

Tonight the wind unravels the moors,
thrashes the roses clotted with ice.
Consider the vaporous ones waiting
among the stars to be born.
Let these fields be planted with melons or wheat.
Let rain fall into the fibrous earth.
Let the fire swallow this body's roads,
throw my ashes into the sea.

Slow Hands

No one could say they were clever or quick,
these knuckles barked on rusted bolts
holding a bad starter motor,
and Lord knows they haven't made me rich
though they've scrounged what they could
from the world's swollen margins,
shoveling ashes from the furnace's throat
onto the driveway's black ice.
Something in the fingerprints never forgets,
smudged indelibly under the surface
the shadows of things carried and stroked:
rake handle, newspaper, child's face, coin.

Slowly they turn the pages now
as night moths ping the screen door
and the palm's lines of prophecy crease
the worn flesh. They beckon me down
from my flickering tower and into the pale
steady tide rising under the broken nails:
husked bent stems wiping tears
or buttoning collars against the wind,
blind whorled pulps turned toward the bread
they will carry up to our mouths.

Lyrical

The spaniel next door yaps at the sparrows,
he yaps at the crows and the mailman,
yaps at the compost pile and the sunflower,
yaps at the rain and the sky. He yaps
at the steps leading down to the creek
where the flax plants bloom high as my waist
and blue flowers force their way up
through small stones the color of night. He
yaps at the garbage truck's back-up beeper,
iron bell song of the priest and the bridegroom,
song of the lone ship, song of the train,
song of the big waves rolling and breaking
over the western reefs. He yaps at the rosebush,
yaps at the fence, song of the sidewalk cracked
in half, the wine bottle resting against the curb,
the neighbor who doesn't come home.

American Wedding

The yarmulke hides the bald spot on my goyische skull
as I watch my new son-in-law's size 13
stomp down on the linen-swathed wine glass.
My daughter looks radiant, no other word
for it, gowned in white satin the color of light.
We're surrounded by Jews dressed in black
like the sea, like the wide streets of Manhattan
whose young men will soon bear me up
on a chair, a floating throne
over the circle clapping and singing.
I've eaten roast duck at the rehearsal dinner,
listened to the cantor's plangent tones,
stood by while the two signed the ornate
ketubah, gold-leafed promise
unscrolled like a map of the world.

My small wan gaggle of distant family
clumps together next to the aisle,
divorced, remarried, adopted, nervous:
our dead father's third wife coughing behind
my stepchildren, ex-wife, half-brothers, motley,
ragged, one nephew wearing a baseball cap.

When the groom lifts the veil from her
delicate temples, I'm thinking someone
should warn them: a future of funerals, car
payments, taxes, kids throwing up in the night.
It's a job you mostly won't know how to do,
your naked arm deep in a jammed kitchen sink,
burnt rinds of eggplant crazily adrift.

Your children will lift their small faces
toward you and give you reason to weep,
and if you manage to stay together
there will be nights you lie down
like strangers back to back
falling away from each other in sleep.

Above us the moon looks speckled, torn,
fluttering over the courtyard
and I'm dazed by the perfume rising up
from this fleshy rose pinned to my worsted lapel.
I'm swallowing down the thick nuptial wine,
getting ready to dance all night.

Poem for Rembrandt

It must have hurt you that winter morning
when the creditors in their stiff wool
descended like so many vultures

clucking and nodding, auctioning off
the paintings and etchings: Dürer,
Rubens, Brueghel, Holbein,

then the helmets, visors, and breastplates,
antique stage props and costume finery,
your African masks, the Carpathian saddle,

Javanese shadow puppets, zithers
and gongs, even the flayed human arm
and hand afloat in a tank of gold fluid.

You buried two wives and three children
and wandered the levees in plague time,
sketchbook under one arm, past the linens

of the newly dead soaked in vinegar and
laid out to dry, while the prodigal world
kept offering itself, a blotched, aging mistress

you never abandoned. You loved what was tattered
and breaking down, the herring pier's pilings
eaten away, worn through by seaworms and ice

or the rash corroding a soldier's cheek, paint
scabbed over, chapped by the wind: Jeremiah
musing on Zion's wreckage or St. Paul entranced

by fatigue, his tan sleeve mottled with lampblack.
In this late self-portrait one hooked vein throbs
below your relentless left eye.

A Love Supreme

I'm hiding an oblong tourmaline ring
I stole from my grandmother's jewel box.
Crouched here among her roses,
the Chicago Peace and the Mister Lincoln,
the American Beauty and Eglantine,
I'm sure I'll never be caught.
My mother's been dead almost a year
and my father's passed out on the couch.
He has no one to help him. Some day
I'll be thirty-five. I'll be drunk
and so angry I'll kick a green trash can
halfway across the airport lobby
when United won't let me board.
I'm late for his funeral already
and my credit card's all used up.
But no one comes to arrest me.
The Hare Krishnas don't ask me
for change, they don't try to sell me
the Bhagavad Gita. Someone
from the Church of John Coltrane
hands me a schedule of services. This
same wet spring Charles Mingus will die
and after him Henry Miller, their music
and language throbbing behind them.
I imagine them waiting there
outside the dead's astral galleries, Miller
smoking a Gauloise, my father
and Mingus, big-shouldered ghosts,
chafing at the delay.
I come to in the back of an airport shuttle
looking out at the Bay's jeweled lights.
Who can predict the world's sudden mercies?
I remember his eyebrow packed with scars
and the broken nose of the security sergeant
who led me outside and onto the bus. Its prow
drives straight through the jagged wind,
its windshield threshes the rain.

from Blue Rust (2012)

Nativity

Long after daybreak they were still trying
to deliver me, the birth blood dropping
on the hospital tiles, glittering under the lights.
I saw my father's corporal's stripes,
his tan army shirt that smelled of tobacco,
I heard the cold wind no one remembers
pouring down out of Canada.

My mother wrapped me up in her robe
fragrant with camphor and sweat,
hushing my desolate howls.
She loved me and she hated me
through those early months
when I wanted everything she had,
and all my father wanted
aside from her warm, pale body,
was to finish his hitch and get the hell
out of the army forever.

Each morning fine grains of salt
glinted like ice on the kitchen table
and like the insatiable mammal I was
I fastened onto her chafed, dark nipples.
They named me Rent Money
because I didn't pay any,
they named me Popsicle, Little Tongue, Gasser.
In August the Japanese surrendered
and he mustered out in Wisconsin.
We headed east in a '38 Studebaker,
its big engine swallowing the miles
of America, wheat fields and highway,
Chicago and Cleveland,
and they named me So Long
It's Been Good to Know You.

Donut Shop Jukebox

Each morning Willis plays checkers
with Eddie, the meth addict 40 days clean
who says he can see the board's white fibers
running from square to square.
Inside it smells of coffee and sugar,
the Shirelles singing "Baby It's You"
and someone taps on the fogged-up
window, late for work, needing
jumper cables. In the fields beyond
where the ditch runs with water
the star thistle opens its stunned
furry leaves, dry needles jabbing the air.

I like the engine roaring to life, a savage
red dogwood shedding its flowers
over the sidewalk, over the fence.
I like your hat with its purple feather,
cheap as a melody, cheap as a wish.

Year of the Ox

Now the town sleeps in its burial robes,
its dim lace of snow trailing over the rooftops,
over the train station, over the struts
on the hotel catwalk
into the dark new moon.

In my boots and my lucky red sweater
I'm going to walk right up to the Ox-King,
touch the bell of his throat, his nostrils,
his thick breath sweet as new grass. . . .
I'm going to ask him about the cold wind
shedding its seedpods and broken stems
over the garden we left behind
where another man and woman
yoked together like us
sleep now on the back porch, the new
bamboo pressing up through the mud.

I can hear the sea calling out
from beyond the jetty, smell the pines
near the flooded-out bridge where today
someone tried to winch an old Volkswagen
up from the swirling waters.
Far down the coast the same west wind
blows through the marshes and river mouth
where my brother's boat rocks on its mooring.
He's the only one awake, modest and reliable,
replacing a frayed hose, tightening the clamps.
He doesn't trust the government
shining his trouble-light into the darkness,
his radio tuned to a satellite
broadcasting through the blue dust of space.

Romance

Soon the cold daylight turns its back
and we crewmen step into the skiff
carrying our groceries and motor oil,
your narrow face a blotch in the fog,
the banks of the estuary loosening
into the channel, horizon angling west.
One more month coming up
watching the moon in its changes
waiting for the salmon to finally arrive,
one more month listening
to seabirds and wind,
listening to you dreaming out loud
about the waitress in Naknek
who called you Honey
when she brought the eggs,
thinking because of your red moustache
you might be one of the Russians
with their slick fiberglass Wegley boats
we never understood how they could afford.

You could have made a life with her, you said
as we watched the corkline
straighten and drift.
You could settle down by her woodstove
turning your back to the road outside,
hidden away in her kitchen,
smelling the spaghetti sauce
like a child or an old man. You could
live easy and die happy, a candle burning
in every window, the blue compass needle
and hands of the clock pointing north
through the field's wavy grass.
You could make your grave in her.

Ode to the Ear

This one's for you, winged skull-blossom
opening into the world, for the gold post held
in your fleshy lobe, for the ledges of blood
swollen inward. Here's
to the whirling sounds of the wind
spilling the dead crepe myrtle leaves
over the hedgerow and garden.
I heard the clock tower's
thick tones reach
into the blue void of Sunday
where I faltered, thinking of winter,
the past with its sunset-rouged face,
its décolletage and long opera gloves,
absinthe and tap water, fireplace
and roof gable, French doors
shedding the rain.

Why should it bring such comfort,
listening to typing in the next room,
the lost notes gathered and tended?
The right ear faces up in the darkness,
here's to its fluids and delicate tympani,
here's to its waxes and hairs,
helpless to close out this rhythmic tapping
it listens and hears and believes.

Divorce

If you were as tired as I was
you too might want to lie down
with the anonymous cats of Santa Cruz
under the gray cars in the parking lot
where the Catholic church
spreads its burnt shadow,
shadow of blood, shadow of thorns—

you could sleep in your overcoat
for maybe three days
like Villon or John Clare
trying to forget the rash on your arms
and the sleek androgynous judge
with a French actress's full upper lip,
his black hair marcelled close
to his skull, his necktie the green
of mosquito repellant.

Now the crickets are throbbing
the ancient psalm of tall grass.
You clasp both hands over your heart
with its pawnshop guitar and fake fur jacket,
its cloth roses sewn end to end,
the turquoise necklace you traded for money
so far from home and too late for autumn,
frozen star lilies bent to the ground.

The Dutch Roll

My father skates on ahead of me,
hands deep in his greatcoat pockets,
brown fedora jammed low.
He's showing me the Dutch Roll,
how to move down the ice for long distances
as they do in the Land of the Silver Skates
shifting one's weight from foot to foot
without thrusting the legs.
I'm proud of the way I can skate,
way better than my brothers.
We're headed for the covered bridge
two miles downstream to the east
and I watch his back. The fur
collar doesn't cover his ears
but he never seems to get cold.
French Creek will not freeze like this
for the rest of the winter we live here,
and tomorrow he'll start drinking again.
Willow branches thin as whips
hang down from the frozen banks,
blackberry canes and pieces of bark
encased in the ice's dark rind.
I smell the wool of my gray muffler,
my eyes are starting to sting. Every
so often the ice booms and cracks
like a rifle going off in a vault
and I hear my own blades
scrape and cut deep on the long thrust
pushing away, having abandoned
the rolling motion because I'm trying now
to catch up. My feet ache from the cold.
I don't want to chicken out and quit.
I don't know how the Dutch kids do it.
The woods are quiet and full of wind
and I think: some things sound better
in books than when you actually do them.
Maybe my father comes back for me

and we turn and skate back upstream together
past the big rocks crusted with snow,
the ice so thick here I can't see through it.

Urban Coyote

In the green dream of spring
I stretch myself out
letting the gray mist hide me
shoving my nose in the garbage pile
chewing egg shells and cheese rinds.
I swallow cellophane, I swallow cat hair,
butcher paper stained dark with fish blood
and run grinning through the blowsy woods
smelling the riverbank's plasma—
I smell the barns and the city dump,
the quail asleep in the tall grass.

In the morning the doctors send over
my lab results: triglycerides and cholesterol,
glucose and prostate antigen,
diets of cold fruit, nuts and water.
I sign the mortgage papers,
I read the bank statement,
I pay the gas bill, I sweep the floor

then in the marshy glycemic night
I lick back the plush fur covering my lips,
I steal whatever can fit in my mouth
under the fat April moon.

Kiski Flats

Soon we'll be driving the black road
I left by, shining with mica,
blistered with tar, the back porch
collapsed where we ate the charred onion rings
watching the Steelers on channel four,
the hatchet sunk deep in the workbench he left
to die in his bed behind the closed door.

It's no crime to be tired of the sun,
to be secretive, hiding your pain.
We peer now into the choppy rooms,
the windows wavy with age and rain.
Let the phone ring forever, let the mail
pile up. Let the dry nest fall apart,
stuck together with last year's mud
jammed in the eaves and shaped like a heart.

Lorca in California

Half the time I'm alone at night
when the raccoons come down to the yard,
rummage collectors, chewers of pine cones.
They sniff the flowers and the possum's carcass,
seething with the white mouths of death.

I grew tired of the poet dressed in black
like the night of no moon, the curved
balconies and colonnades, hothouse Madrid's
old lacquer. I couldn't care less about Dalí now,
his glass clocks and corpses, his giant
moustache, or Buñuel's fake lenses
and flickering lights, all that bright equipment.

I want to stay here forever
in this ramshackle hut with its roses and dog hair,
its peach tree blossoms, pollen and dust,
the compost fuming out back by the fence.
My new lover works on the tuna boats,
he comes home smelling of old rope
and anchovies, money in both his front pockets,
shiny blue scales on his boots.

Blow Job Cole Slaw

"A woman will give you anything,"
T.K. would advise, "if you know
how to cook." He'd lean against
the scarred cutting block, sleeves
rolled up past the elbow, chopping
the purple and ivory cabbage
we could only get once in a while
into narrow shreds. Some nights
I still dream of the salmon boat,
the picking-bin littered with black tape
and hanging twine, sunset turning
dim like a weld over the Bering Sea.

We chewed the fine roughage
gratefully along with our noodles
and corned beef hash, the net
a loose skirt flaring down
over the stern roller's horns.
So much vinegar, so much mayonnaise:
night coming up from the shifting depths,
its dark veils unwinding, its unbraided hair,
floating half a mile up the cutbank, we
slept in our damp socks and sweatshirts,
we opened our cramping, feverish hands.

Half Made

Something half made like the love poem
left behind in the front seat
or the youngest child who keeps turning
to leave, his nicotine fingers and widow's peak.
Something half made like this high rise,
jackhammer breaking the curb,
its terrace abandoned, then planted again
with lilacs and clumped, fleshy herbs.
Something half made like a wedding blanket
nobody thinks will last or it could be
the thin skin of the past:
counting the capillaries and veins,
the tiny bones in your feet,
even at night the blood pulses,
the iron planet hums in the heat.
Something half made
like the song of the crow,
the marriage vows given and taken
even at night, blow by blow.

For Weldon Kees

Nobody here thinks you really died
having spied you alone on the sidewalk

in New Orleans, full brown moustache
and narrow shoes, the long cuffs
of your linen shirt turned back.

To become as clean as you are—
body of salt, body of glass—
the rest of us would have to sleep
under the desert stars for a year:

Mexico with its funeral horse,
its housefly and cactus, its lottery ticket.

To become as quiet as you are
we would have to originate ourselves
as we do in the fall, watching
more daylight vanish each day,

the crows webbed in shadow
on the garage roof,
the dusky ruinous sunset.

It's the way you lean against
the hotel balcony
sipping a tall grapefruit juice
having grown tired of the sound

of the fountain, dead leaves
blowing past in the street.

You are nobody's father's ghost
spending evenings alone in your room
watching the fan blades turn overhead
listening to Chopin and Brahms.

Though your absence makes
a dark sea around you
you are not Odysseus,
you are nobody's father.

Day of the Dead

Last night the owl swooped low overhead
and dropped a torn hen carcass
on the neighbor's roof,
red feathers scattered, feet hanging down
which they've left sprawled on the shingles
like some occult sign
hoping to see him return,
and here come the children up the walk
through the pine mulch and drizzle
into my yellow porch light:
Count Dracula with porcelain fangs,
a five-year-old Cleopatra
wearing a vest with gold trim.

All day I've tried to ignore the ice cream truck
jingling its bell past the cemetery
where the tramp in his watch cap sings to himself
like a mad general or movie director:
Jean Cocteau letting the stage dust
filter the twilit underworld
where death looks like a torch singer
who wants to make love to Orpheus,
or Sam Peckinpah with his bullets and dynamite
getting ready to blow up the water tower,
the script in one hand and a gin in the other
keeping an eye out for beauty.

They held my friend's funeral yesterday
out west under the night's long windows,
under its dying stars,
my friend who didn't trust doctors or cops,
who left behind him the green country roads
and the tilted black streets of town,
who left behind the pale flower
whose delicate roots they never could find
blooming inside his brain.

The children paw through the sugar skulls,
their big sister hanging back in the shadows
whispering into her cell phone
like a homicide detective,
the vampire count and Egyptian queen,
history's most famous suicide.
Listen to the night freight coming down,
its engines, its wheels, its sacks of ripe grain,
its gray rats grown fat by the iron tracks,
its love-moan traveling back through the rain.

Nightbound

Your knuckles relax and your hands
open slowly each time you enter
the house of sleep
which you will never own,
its black windows shining
on the black lawn
smelling of cloves,
feathers and ink, the flakes
of soot collecting ceaselessly
over the smoldering cookfire,
perfect whorled thumbprint left behind
on the water glass by the sink.

Nothing to hear or see or hold onto,
blue rust floating away from your
touch, dark mosses crumbling under
your tongue, nothing to carry back,
curled on one side with your knees drawn up:
father, mother, grandmother, uncle,
naming your dead one by one.

Ocean

Where we swam alone under the skiff,
its green shadow knife-shaped
far overhead,
ribbons of seaweed,
the soundless engine,
soundless the shouts
and the wind
shouldering the surf's
white flowers,
water snuffed up our sinuses,
the beach-fire cinders
like phosphorous at night,
jeans caked with salt,
the funeral moon.
Beach with dark rocks and saw grass,
winter keeps coming down from the north,
each grain of sand ticks underfoot,
each star whines overhead.
Beach with dark rocks, the long boats
drift, the children leave home, no one
speaks. Each night lying down
in our sea-wrack, each day waking
into our skin.

       . . .

Come close and whisper the names
of the living, names of the dead returning,
sleepwalkers holding their hands out,
litter of sea-straw and sand like dark metal,
song of arriving and going away.
Forgive me my pride, inexplicable
under the circumstances,
storm coming in tomorrow night,
old rain gear dotted with herring scales.
I ate the kelp blossom

down to the root,
eel flesh and crab flesh, I ate the shark meat,
octopus, yellow fin, scallops, clams, delicate flesh of the lobster.

. . .

What was the song she sang,
the sea lion cow asleep on a rock
near Point Reyes?
I hear the deep halls of water
filling up on the ebb
as she turns over, sighing into the algae,
slides back into the tide.
I squatted still in the autumn sand
thinking of red roe and black hair,
women gone down into themselves,
funky, brash,
croaking and thrashing
eyes staring blind as glass.

. . .

Don't be afraid to go sailing out,
don't think of riptides,
storms,
huge seas
risen over the flybridge,
threads of fire,
the jaws of a wolf eel
slithering out of the trawl.

. . .

One summer night the fisherman told us
he'd run aground in the river mouth, hull
mired deep in black mud. He said he saw
the hour of his birth, the swamp slowly
filling with light, kelp stretched out
like a vestment covering the flanks of the marsh,
the sea's wretched age, monstrous and fecund,

hair full of dead leaves, rayed petals clustered,
shoals of dark gravel exposed.
Inside the wheelhouse one candle burning,
bunks tilted stiffly to starboard.

He told us sometimes he'd rather be dead
than face the gray rooming house
and a day job, his heart like iron
remembering the sea and staring
at frayed pallets stacked in a warehouse
smelling of creosote. All
the gathered rubbings of shore trash
making him sneeze and itch:
stove ashes, moth wings stuck to the screens,
dog hair, spider webs, elm pollen.

                    . . .

Always the sound of the hull slapping down
into the wave trough, always
the caulked seam of metal
its wet patch turning to sugar,
saltwater seeping down the spine,
miles offshore the snowy moonlight,
miles below the abyssal trench
where a creature with no eyes
and glandular poison sends its forked signals
into the murk, sleepless predator
prowling the shadows,
turning its stomach inside out,
vulnerable, sunk in its hunger.

                    . . .

This time of year you can hate the snow,
freezing the tie-up lines, coating the wharves,
falling into the jagged surf.
If you wait long enough you can ride
into town on the boom truck, its tire chains

shredding the crust, the engine
so noisy no one can speak,
the driver grinding it up into second
frowning with grease on his knuckle.

No place will be open now
except for the sad bar, barren of women,
except for the motel near the dunes
with its flocked wallpaper
and rusty heater that moans
in the night like a tired swan.
The next day no one will look
in your eyes, transparent stranger
belonging to no one,
not the children sledding on cardboard
down through the frozen parking lot,
not the waitress humming a song
you wish you could remember . . .

if she asked you about your family
you could show her their silhouettes
in a drop of saltwater from Wingaersheek Beach
you keep in a jar by the window.
You could show her
the rags of evening
fluttering over the waves
and a sofa's blond fabric
dotted with burns
like the skin of a mangy leopard.
You could show her the plaster
Egyptian sculptures,
emblems of dynasty fallen,
its copy of Queen Nefertiti's face,
the nose broken off,
her green headdress wound high
into the domed light
sifting down on the sink.

Thy sea is so great
and my boat is so small
stamped in metal over the door—
my thin hands gripping the shovel
and loosening dirt in the garden,
the restless claws of the ocean
turning the pebbles and rocks and sand,
tumbling the chitin and shell fragments
ceaselessly each day and night forever:
Quaternary, Cretaceous, Jurassic, Cambrian
onto the shores of this world.

from Kingdom (2017)

Time-Poem

No one will tell me
where the horses have gone
who rested under the oak trees
especially the black one with mottled lips
who would hum to himself
when I stroked his chest fur
nicked up by barb wire and covered
with flies, beneath which his huge
and sleepless heart
carried him into the summer,
his ghost now grazing the roadside
this night before the Florida Derby.

The pasture's a canebrake of ancient kudzu
laid down and braided with rusted fence,
the road a wide strip of moonlit ashes
leading away from the barn
where my friend makes his sculptures
of clay and branched iron,
unchanged by wind and time

though Jupiter hangs low overhead,
like us unable to escape the hours.
It's two in the morning on the coast
of the moon but here it's just midnight
and the sleepers open their arms
to the sound of 5,000 horses
driving the big train south from Monroe
dragging the long cars mile after mile,
its engineer like an aging king
watching the clock, one hand on the throttle,
the howl of the whistle under the stars,
trapped and burning.

Muse

Who can tell how she got here
in her headdress and midnight braids,
drifting ashore in a black skiff
and planting the seeds of 2012
she stole from the early Mayans
next to the golf course pond
where the young boys in Phoenix
go fishing at night for the shadowy cats
that lie just off the bottom
in their spiky whiskers and rayed fins.
When they hook a big one, they snap
a quick trophy-photo
keeping an eye out for the watchman.

No one can tell when she'll be back
carrying her cup of embalming fluid
and her book about primitive shame
though we wait for her in the paisley chair,
entering each evening quietly
with someone sick in the other bed
of a gray motel where she might
be found, random police sirens
strobing the neighborhood.

But she is not thinking of beauty or death,
only the wet shoes and denim,
the beer cans collected and desert stars
shining like salvaged metal
and the big fish released
sinking back to the bottom
to feed on the muddy stems—
its strange flat head and narrow lips,
its naked, electric-blue skin.

Semi-Retired

Sometimes the most I do all day
is wander the grocery aisles in a trance
looking for a deal on yellow onions
or a half pound of lunch meat.
Back home I watch
the city's backhoe
digging a trench in the street.
This is the life, I say to myself,
whiff of coffee and cotto salami,
whiff of broken-up asphalt.

At seventy I keep waking up
next to my father's corpse,
supine in necktie and herringbone vest,
blue shirt spattered with wine.
Get out of my way, I tell him,
watching the nurse arrive
sent by the new insurance company
to measure my vitals and blood.

I try to keep quiet during the week
though I love my small-time anonymous self
breaking jars in the trash bin
destructive and silent and grandiose,
lost in its dreams of ashes and theft
and speaking about them to no one.

And my body seems like a sister,
sister of fluids and oxygen,
sister of sleep in the afternoon.
I roll up my sleeve and hold out
my arm to the home-nurse resting
her thumb on my wrist,
looking down at her watch
like an overweight angel of mercy
listening to the blood
running back to the heart,
telling me to breathe and let go.

One Day

Everything shimmers
with the sound of the train
rattling over the bridge
especially the ears and nostrils and teeth
of the horse riding out
to the pasture of breath
where the long freight runs
on diesel fuel
that used to run on coal.
I keep listening
for the crickets and birds
and my words fall down below.

I mistook the train for a thunderstorm,
I mistook the willow tree
for a home, it's nothing to brag about
when you think of it
spending this time all alone.
I wandered into the hay field
and two ticks jumped in my hair,
they dug in my scalp
and drank up my blood
like the sweet wine of Virginia,
then left me under the Druid moon
down here on earth in the kingdom.

Courtly

No matter the high-flown improbable phrases,
the tinned fish and flowers, lipstick
and wine—no matter Venice's
gimcrack cornices
holding their arms apart in the night
or the red dahlias swaying on long stems
walloping each other in the summer wind.

It isn't the blue rocks at low tide
or the long grass by the sea wall,
lady of time and dried white flowers,
lady of distant rain

who wanders off looking for a book of matches
along the road near the coffee shop
built to look like a chateau
and spattered with bird shit
where gulls and ravens
like the Hollywood movies
have feasted for over a century
on the corpses of Lancelot and Keats.

Nobody knows what it's cost you
to keep facing up to the world like this
with its airport exhaust and chalk dust,
both of us tired, both of us cold,
trying to talk with the professors
and lonely for California.

I bring these today to the door
of your dream, as close
as I can approach:

saltwater to heal your sinuses,
coffee with soy milk and coconut,
blanket to warm your shoulders,
bag of blue ice for your spine.

Ronnie: 1954–2013

Ronnie's eyes are bloodshot and steady
under his iron-colored hair
and the wind keeps making mine
blink and tear
outside the noon Meeting
while he tells me about the twenty-dollar
Tuesday Night Life-Drawing Class,
about quitting art school years ago
out west in California
to become a private detective,
the same year Nixon got re-elected
only to resign from office:
no more Bischoff and Diebenkorn,
no more mute wisdom of canvas and line,
no more Joan Brown and David Park,
his green skiff in the estuary,
picnic rain on the banks

and if the body is the world's last hotel,
its vestibules worn by time,
he will have checked out early
and be waiting outside alone
relaxing in one of those woven blue chairs,
in no big hurry to go anywhere
and admiring with his painter's eye
the earth's accidental beauty
which never can last—
the daylight moon overhead
as well as the splashes of last night's rain
which have settled the clouds of tree pollen
into pale green aqueous streaks
the color of ancient burnished metal
on the dark flat stones of the terrace.

Field

I sat down in the yellow chair
in the hush before the rain
watching the women walking together
through the glass door in their fulsome skin.
It was better than sleeping,
better than gin
with the immense heaven far overhead
the color of lead or beaten tin.

I saw their shirts loosely darkened
after the small drops began,
I saw their ribs and hips and hair
and it looked as though they were floating
across the electric air.

The election raged on in the cities
and death came in the night
for the famous judge—
whatever it is that resists transformation
must have abandoned him—
maybe the iron in the blood.

And then the rain opened its silver wings
beating down on the grasses
combed back by the wind
and the trees and plants
with their roots and seeds,
their blossoms and delicate limbs.

Language

Her fallen arch which you bend across
kissing the knobs of her feet, the patchy glaze

of her toenails rendering you half drunk
in the heat. Why not forget your mother's voice

scattered like ashes in the surf, the saltwater
trenches and ocean caverns' violent fiery birth.

Shot through with holes, the place you were born
buzzing with locusts, hornets and flies

a gray dove nests below your window
listening to her mate's anonymous cry,

the estuary spread like an aging hand,
the paring-knife moon and two-lane bridge

and your lips which are grazing her ankle now
the tongue's flat muscle, the palate's ridge

echoing the doorway of childhood's
language, its trances of taste and smell,

the sounds formed somewhere back of the teeth
and shaped in the mouth's vestibule.

The Poetry-Body

for Kwame

The youngest won't fall asleep
though he keeps resting his head on the table
next to his empty plate.
These are the jewels of his
half-open eyes bewitched by the pale
blossoming spines of the centerpiece flowers
no one remembers the names of—
these are the sparks flying up
from the fire and the night
pressing in on the windows.

I know by now the harsh stillness
of a winter night by the beach,
the moon half hidden
low and dim
and sometimes I think
poetry has failed me,
the nights gone by and chances missed
all breathing deeply beside me—
"a fluttering of feathers"
you called it,
this soft body that consumes everything
especially our failures
carrying something under its tongue
it is not going to show
to anyone.

Girlfriends

They come jittering into her life from the past,
brunette like her mother, wiry
and tense, wearing garments black
as anthracite chopped from the city's heart.
Complaint rises like music or smoke
past the elegant lamps of their faces
as they settle their fringe and nail polish
onto our secondhand couch: men, mostly,
but the theme could be anything,
children, money, uterine cramping,
low brilliant choruses of damage and pain.

They tell her their dreams, of roses
and falling. They point to the crow's feet
deepening each year above
the wings of their cheekbones.

In the one painting my mother left
when she died, the waves are breaking
over Folly Cove. All night they will break
in the autumn dark, while one friend sleeps
holding onto her boy-lover and another
drives south through the rain-soaked hills
bound for her sister's third wedding. They
carry the yoke of the city's blue lights
easily back toward morning. They feel
their bodies grow beautiful, the night sky
smoothing their faces and hair. Nobody
needs to tell them death's hands
keep opening over the road.

Eclipse

Linden branches and narrow streets,
frost and ice on the full solstice moon

the first in 300 years this day
to suffer a total eclipse

though there's plenty of snow and daylight
yet to fall through the branches

each day lasting a minute longer
all the way up to spring.

Now you can make a wish
for the new year, now you

can lie awake in the dawn
listening to the plow's hydraulic blade

and the old dog that howls at the stars.
It can be hard to sleep in America

land of ceaseless wind and weather,
granite slabs and the sea breaking over them

traveling thousands of miles.
But you are the curious unfaltering one,

alive in the rouged earth-shadow
who combs out the knots in the dog's gray fur

and kisses the lover in the hidden mouth
and knows the moon will come back.

Oxygen and Acetylene

for Steve

As I stand in the door, talking on
about poetry and courtly love—
the unattainable woman
and the delicate Arabic forms,
he keeps looking past me
at the small bat that swoops
through the sawdusted air
and shits on the drill press
and bandsaw,
the welding tanks and the torch
he got at a bargain price back home
from a man going through a divorce.

Why Women Live Longer

You can hear two thin minor chords
through the wall and the song
in a broken falsetto
as you lie on the couch
half out of your body
unable to feel your feet—
dead leaves blowing off the tin roof
just ahead of the rain—
then something about a coal mine,
something about a train.

You don't like her to see you like this
though she knows you well,
your socks fallen down and the rough hair
all worn away from your shins
which are shiny now
like an old man's
which is what you're becoming
this afternoon, listening to faint music,
watching the shadows drift
down the gray ceiling, stained
like a liver X-ray.

She comes in the house with her girlfriend,
they soldier along through the desert of time.
They rub lotion into their aging calves
speaking of shoes, speaking of hair,
the tea roses climbing the mailbox.
If you could you would visit
your father's ashes, long since
scattered on Lighthouse Beach,
no matter the feeling of rootlessness,
of night coming on and the early stars
almost out of reach.

Night

Nobody wants to fall asleep
watching the stars burn like trash fires,
listening to the big waves smoke
down the rocks,
nobody wants to sleep.

My Pelikan 800 fountain pen,
green with a faint gold stripe,
lost with my hundred-proof memory,
my sea flat as glass,
its kelp leaves and poppies.

Now I watch the women
dressed in black—black shoes,
black pants, long hair falling
over their hands and wrists.
They stay awake far into the night
writing their scattered poems,
sisters of the half-empty wine jar,
of childhood lost
in the coastal fog and the lapsed
Catholic funeral flowers.

Nobody thinks of going to sleep
now that the streetcars are silent,
now that the dew seeps
into the grass.
I came west in my twenties
looking for work,
driving straight into the setting sun
and now I'll take anything:
a pencil stub and a cheap
cardboard notebook
somebody gave me for nothing.

Valentine

It's February in North Carolina,
the day before Valentine's Day,
and we listen to the elegant waves
quiet and monstrous, grinding away

at the sand's fractured layers
of feldspar and quartz, the dunes'
dark gray cactus and pampas grass,

the incoming tide we walk beside
drinking take-out coffee,
stooping down every now and then
to pick up a shell or a smooth piece of glass

and talking about an old friend,
now sailing a southern ocean
who doesn't want to come back to land

more afraid of contentment
and the slow trances of age
than the elements of the deep,
maybe thinking it would be no great outrage
to die on the water, like falling asleep—

tired like the rest of us
and not willing to admit it:
even the wars of baseball,
even love's politics,
even the slab-sided salmon
hauled up for years on his decks—

and maybe dreaming like Coleridge
of rocking forever in the blue void
like a floating abandoned wreck.

I make us turn back when we reach the pier
weary of walking, wanting to lie down,

our footprints already disappearing
under the shrouds of foam.

One of the things I like about you
is the way you can leave things alone

with your hat pulled low over your hair
and your face partly hidden below,
stepping pigeon-toed next to me
watching the distant whitecaps flare

and the strong wings of seabirds
relentless and young
beating high up in the air.

Patience

How long must we wait, composer,
for the slender moon
to shine down its light
on piano keys turned yellow with age,
for the living, ordinary notes
of the nocturne
to divide the crimes of pretending
from the crime of falling asleep?

I'm afraid of the oil
rising into the Gulf
where the drilling rig has exploded,
the black snake climbing the fence post
to swallow the catbird's eggs.

How long till the fat man lying back
in the next room
holding the guitar to his chest
like a piece of wreckage
keeping him afloat
opens his mouth to sing?

You reach out your hand
like the messiah of pawnshops,
of late-night trains
coming down from the north,
the flute in its dark red velvet case
beginning to tarnish and fade . . .

You reach out your other hand
over the brickwork,
wide awake in the dazzle of spring,
coal dust fallen like pollen
on the window glass and the shade.

Artist Colony

You'd like to be home
watching reruns of *Kojak*
busting crooks in the big city canyons,
cruising an unmarked V-8 Lincoln,
his stingy-brim slantwise on his shaved scalp—
a .45 in his coat—
pulling a lollipop
from his thick lips
and saying, "Who loves ya, baby?"

It's fun to think of him,
now deceased, enjoying
an easy old age from residuals,
maybe some golf,
a little backgammon,
more likely a day at the track
where he once owned a thoroughbred
named Telly's Pop
that won the Del Mar Futurity
though you lost forty bucks
when you bet him to win
the same year at Bay Meadows.

And now you sit quietly
in the large common room
listening to the music of two composers
younger than most of your children:
music of glass and magnetized metal,
music of searchlights in outer space.

Outside, the finches keep eating seeds
from the spiked orange crowns
of the candle flowers
and the black horse in the pasture
you fed all those apples and carrots
no longer seems to remember you.

Ancestral

Sometimes the bent ghost of my father
holding a dead Pall Mall in its teeth
walks the sandy track to the beach
he called "my garden"
where he would lie on his stomach reading
a book about astronomy
or the history of music,
maybe a seed catalog—
the channel a deep blue
passing the lighthouse,
split slabs of granite
heaped up on the shore,
saltwater sparkling in the cuts.

I like it when the flood tide
surges in once a month
overcoming the land,
seawater rising under the face
of the pale stone
gazing down from the heavens,
veiling her dark side from us
where some people claim
entire cities exist.

I like to write with this space pen
given to me by a friend,
the same one the astronauts use.
I fall asleep with the milky way
wrapped around my shoulders.
I like the burned methane clouds
and the black threads of iron
sunk deep in the stars, and the earth
where it's sometimes cast into bells—
bells of the evening, bells of death,
bells of some ruthless joy—
iron that floats like salt in the bloodstream,
plasma inheritance, proteins and enzymes,

two million red cells every second
born in the body's jubilant fire,
the deep cells of the marrow.

End of the World

December 21, 2012

Everyone's still waking up this day
listening to the Angeles bells
or maybe listening to neighborhood gunfire:
here at the end of the Mayan calendar
with its cycles of Venus
and Lords of the Night

the cold wind
gusting out of the north
so the wren puffs its feathers

and the lights on the blue spruce,
splinters of ice
flicker and burn by the window.

Season of holly berries and dead leaves,
darkness and distant stars,

the sweet time taken
to build a fire

each stroke of the broom
sweeping the hearth,
each sheet of newsprint
with its gambler's heart:

the day's price of gold,
its lies and wars
crumpled into a ball,

each stick laid in and tilted up,
ingots of white pine, maple and oak

and the smell of burnt sap
rising into the smoke . . .

Everyone's still waking up
in their beds or a ditch

or the one metal bench
under the airport's cold steel roof
looking up at the lights of the Milky Way
which the Mayans called the Crocodile Tree . . .

and I fall in love in the morning
thousands of miles below

watching your feet through the doorway
walking out into the first day of winter

with its broken sunlight
and haphazard weather,
its frozen mud and new snow

its blackened roses and jaguar tears
falling for 5,000 years.

New Poems

Pablo and Me

In California it's laundry day
and I'm dreaming of Pablo Neruda

who's ordering lobster and crab
in a small hotel by the sea,
the shells piling up
and the wine bottles,
vessels of deepest green
settled amidst the gorgeous wreckage

interrupting himself now and then
to give directions to the beach
or the Ladies Room
or to order more wine

and I tell him this is no way
for a humble Communist to behave
who spoke truth to power
when the miners went on strike
and he says what do I know,
I'm not the one who hid from the law
months at a time
and had to escape into Argentina
horseback under cover of night

so now I'm afraid he'll stop talking to me
but he says not to worry
and I believe him
that we can have cakes
with nuts and whipped cream
and then I can ask
if he'll come back once more
and read his extravagant poetry.

In the laundry room next to the kitchen
the clothes are thrashing around
like poems that refuse to be abandoned,

politically conscious or not,
inside the washer's ferocious orbit:

T-shirts and red bandana
wedged in the Levi's zippers.
They keep dissolving ancestral dirt
from worn-out collars and fraying crotches
bunched up in their threadbare seams
and I'm stranded here at the kitchen table
down to my last pair of shorts

the smell of beets roasting in the oven
smoky and rank as the grave . . .

and this is not Isla Negra, with its mermaid
goddess looming out of the wall,
its Hindu carvings and glass butterflies,
its studio floor paved with seashells.

This is the kind woman's kitchen,
a soft rain falling outside the door
where I dream of the Chilean poet,

his skin of dark felt and his eyes of water
gazing down into the sea.

Corvus

My wife thinks the crows
are talking to her
with their midnight beaks
and ragged feathers
and maybe she sees the sky though their eyes,
the reef of dark storm cloud
off to the west, the flutter
of deep laughter under her breast
and under their bandaged squawks

and I'm thankful for the privilege
of memory and thought
for I still wear the scar on my hand
from setting steel steps
onto the trailers
my first week in Dead Horse
near Prudhoe Bay,
back when we still had an Arctic,
where a can of soda
left outside for three minutes
would freeze into solid ice:

ice in the air, ice in the sky,
ice in our nostrils and under our eyes:
who knew some day we would miss it?
Ice-tears and ice-spit
ice-piss and ice-shit
so cold you couldn't smell,
glare-ice like the front yard of hell

and the first living creature a raven
perched on the trash burner
with a voice like bent tin
under the delicate rose-colored sun
which never lifted above the horizon
circling all day like a dim lamp
along the gray edge of heaven.

Some Days

Some days we sit at the kitchen table
watching the dark liquid meal
trickle down the dim plastic tube
ported into his gut.
Some days we walk a good ways
up the shore
to the Rosie the Riveter Museum
looking out for an egret or night heron.
The halyards rattle, wind of November, smoke
from the fires in the vineyards and valleys
finally swept from the air.

Some days, you might say,
better than others: the photo
someone gave us of E. E. Cummings,
light fedora pushed back from his face
looking down at us
like a Mediterranean prince—
and how do you like your blue-eyed boy:
my brother's ribs showing under his skin
crisscrossed with veins and capillaries,
his small ankles motley and swollen,
a strange authority in his expression now,
unaffected by the tumor in his cheek.
He tells me to stop rubbing his feet
to just sit still and talk to him—
so I tell him about the impeachment hearings
while the refrigerator hums
and he drowses in his blue chair.

Sometimes his eyes flutter open
as though one of the mansions
in the Father's house
has come down close through the night
and he can peer into its windows.

Forgiveness

I took a sip of black tea and honey
crossing the bay at night
on the way to his last Christmas service
and he asked me, What are you drinking,
bound as he was to the feeding tube,
his mouth full of cancer-phlegm.

He was wrapped up
in his coat and scarf,
the Greek fisherman's cap
he often wore
and the tumor in his cheek
hardly smelled at all,
thanks to numerous chemical scrubbings
and a fresh dressing of cotton and gauze.

Also there was a cold rain
stinging the windshield
and a fitful December wind
gusting in from the west.
It wouldn't be the King Tide coming in,
not for another three weeks.
It wasn't the Solstice
or a falling star
or a penumbral eclipse.

It was my brother's cool
fine-boned hand
resting on mine in the front seat
for one calm, deliberate moment
high above the dark water.

Fayetteville Street

When you awake high over the city
with the March wind hammering the glass
and the invisible drummer

we would sometimes hear
while the winter night slowly passed
with his sticks and can

an upside-down bucket
they use for house-paint
and drywall mud

working its hard bottom and rim—
single-strokes, paradiddles,
drags, four-four time

the good beat deep in his blood.

Can you spare a few minutes
if not a dime
and sit with me on the balcony

listening to the rhythm linger and fade,
its wrists and knuckles,
its gloves with no fingers

and no place to sleep till day.

Mistletoe

It's the morning after the big rain,
the daffodils twinkling in the alley
and the sky still gray

through the giant maple branches
where we can see a clump of mistletoe
way up near the crown

and you wonder
because you are always curious,
how do they get it down?

The internet says
they use a shotgun to harvest it
or else they explore a swamp

where the plant digs its rapacious roots,
its *haustoria*, its mojo hand,
into the bark of an oak,

then lives off its water and nutrients
the same way it does on dry land
with its smooth oval leaves

and death-waxy berries,
a goddess's pale tears shed for her son,
issue of her divine flesh and blood

struck down in his youth by an arrow
made from its delicate wood.

And now people kiss beneath it at Christmas
or beside the bonfire at solstice

their mouths together, enmeshed for a time,
as though willing to host one another's life force
and testing the acid and alkaline—

and maybe we should get married again,
this time with music and a big white cake,
the plush stars shining dim and opaque
and a honeymoon riding a train.

Meadow

My father is a lowland meadow,
his tall rushes bend in the wind

over the vetch and sedge grass hay
and the pernicious dandelion

with its tough single taproot
that inches down through the clay.

He opens his heart
to the April rain

and the horses he loved
when he was here

to lean up against and whisper and stroke
inside their silken ears.

At night he sees Venus
hanging close to the moon

and he doesn't care
about ideas or sleep

or how far he had to roam
drifting through space and the silent deep

caressing the dawn's irresistible face
following the way back home.

Ventriloquist

for Marvin

If I wandered long enough in the desert
maybe I could be clean again
like an astronaut in training
or the sands of the moon.
If I could open the doors to my heart
and give it the full control,
sleepless driver with stents in its pipes,
a lump in my throat,
my luxurious soul
that keeps its eyes open and has no fear
of the gray ashen sky and smoky air
which is why I ask you this morning my dear,
are you going to the store all alone?

With only your busted lip for a shield,
the dusty cornet and old marathon shoes,
the dried-up wreath of purple magnolia
brought down from the attic
with dark stiffened leaves
the color of death,
whose shadow arrived on delicate feet
like the man at the food bank,
who took delivery without a word
of the five cases of liquid meals—
and knew why my brother
could no longer use them—

or like your late poems whose lines
would run over, then
partway across, hanging down—
sentences full of proverbs and mercury—
in a voice you would tell us
belongs to someone who knows you quite well
and is not exactly your own.

Venetian Siesta

I know I'm getting away with a crime
stretched out on the couch
and listening to rain
making a hole in the afternoon
through which I can drift slowly away

for sleep is sometimes
just as delicious
as grilled polenta and creamy white fish.
So I give up my hands,
my tears and my face,
the smells of tar,
damp rope and mud,
the late-slanted light of November
rippling below on the gondola wood

and then I count backwards from 27
trying to pretend I'm Wallace Stevens,
he of the freakish intellect
and the taste of a ruthless
wandering gourmet
who rummages in the mystical kitchen
in search of oranges and café espresso
or a blown-glass peacock
or a Byzantine horse
cast in some delicate metal.

He speaks of the world,
how it's changed by art
and bread you can't eat
powdered with light
where someone is toasting
their mother's health
and someone is writing a letter to death
which makes things beautiful
in its way
and also makes everyone the same

as laughter does
or the late autumn rain.

Epithalamion

It was a hotel wedding
in the days of early spring

with a sheer white veil and roses
a 24-karat ring

and everyone wanted to climb the stairs
to dance with the bride

in her plush brassiere
her bitter garter and snowy dress

bearing them up like a sacrifice
with their ballast of fallen tears.

Someone told me her toenails
were painted indigo blue

the color of night or a raincloud
inside her seed-pearl shoes

while the band played on
full of nostalgia

above Division Street's misty cars
for weddings come and weddings gone.

They played the mambo
and "Pennies from Heaven,"

their black tuxedos embroidered with stars
like Sirius, Rigel or Ganymede,

Jupiter's largest moon
with its hidden ocean sixty miles deep

under the silicate's shadowy plains,
under its curved icy grooves.

And here was no ancient mariner,
earthbound, stopping a guest at the door

with a crooked tale of wandering
over some cruelty that happened before

for this was a ritual entirely made new
with vows both silent and spoken

though everyone present already knew
each day they could be broken

for the stairs going up are the stairs going down
from the attic to the dirt cellar floor

and far beyond, the river would flow on
over its distant shore.

Memorial Day Meditation

I want to cross over the invisible line
a passageway back
through the root of the nose
into the skull or the depth of the gut

where there's no memory
of tracer bullets
and mortar fire shaking the earth,
not in my cells or my nerve endings
thanks to the brothers
I never see any more

Henry, wounded in the siege
at Khe Sanh
or Sherwood who stared in my eyes
one morning and told me how useless
it was to resist
or the boys in the Dodge van
with its poster of Hendrix,
its porthole windows and deep shag carpet
who gave me a ride across Wyoming
smoking their killer ganja.

Today the long pond shaped like a footprint
flows through the leaves of watercress
and over the dam made of stones and wood
where the turtle is resting
alone in the sun
with his delicate claws and reptile blood
his shell etched with time's abiding laws
and nothing is forbidden to him.

Masks

I refuse to wear one
in the great outdoors
walking by the sea in the live air
or under the cypress trees growing near
though sometimes I want to turn away
from the pale sky
with its solitary plane trailing through,

and one big crow high up on the wing
carrying something white in its beak,
a solstice messenger
who knows how to talk
but doesn't know how to sing

over these beloved latitudes
where the rabbit drums his back foot
before springing away through the tall grass,
since these are the holidays
of the pandemic
and nothing makes too much sense.

I need a lawyer to interpret my dreams
and a long train to carry the dead,
the part that's unseen and the part
that's unsaid,
except for the sound of December wind
and the smell of pine resin
and rabbit's breath
which has gone underground again.

Affluence

What I inherited
was the dim world of the left eye
clouded over in the photos
left behind in her desk:
my mother holding me
in the backyard, Rockport, 1947
where they struggled to make the rent.
I can barely remember her,
wool scarf binding the cloud of her hair,
tortoise shell glasses askew in the wind,
the sea off Back Beach
like a field of wrecked metal,
gray light shining within.

When they take off the cataracts
the daylight floods in,
sharpening the leaf points and wisps
of tall grass and I open my mouth
to the chill air
as you lead me back to the car,
tell me about the damson plum jam
you read about in Joan Didion:
farmer's market, four bucks a jar.

I look at your straw hat's bent crown,
your hands with their slender bones,
I see the small ruby chip the jeweler
made into a ring one Christmas
when I couldn't afford a whole stone
and I know we're one with the ants in the garden,
late November, the last days of fall,
down in the dirt with the deer tracks,
the lichens and stems and root-hairs,
the abundance of all things small.

2007
Trick Pear, Suzanne Cleary
So I Will Till the Ground, Gregory Djanikian
Black Threads, Jeff Friedman
Drift and Pulse, Kathleen Halme
The Playhouse Near Dark, Elizabeth Holmes
On the Vanishing of Large Creatures, Susan Hutton
One Season Behind, Sarah Rosenblatt
Indeed I Was Pleased with the World, Mary Ruefle
The Situation, John Skoyles

2008
The Grace of Necessity, Samuel Green
After West, James Harms
Anticipate the Coming Reservoir, John Hoppenthaler
Convertible Night, Flurry of Stones, Dzvinia Orlowsky
Parable Hunter, Ricardo Pau-Llosa
The Book of Sleep, Eleanor Stanford

2009
Divine Margins, Peter Cooley
Cultural Studies, Kevin A. González
Dear Apocalypse, K. A. Hays
Warhol-o-rama, Peter Oresick
Cave of the Yellow Volkswagen, Maureen Seaton
Group Portrait from Hell, David Schloss
Birdwatching in Wartime, Jeffrey Thomson

2010
The Diminishing House, Nicky Beer
A World Remembered, T. Alan Broughton
Say Sand, Daniel Coudriet
Knock Knock, Heather Hartley
In the Land We Imagined Ourselves, Jonathan Johnson
Selected Early Poems: 1958-1983, Greg Kuzma
The Other Life: Selected Poems, Herbert Scott
Admission, Jerry Williams

2011
Having a Little Talk with Capital P Poetry, Jim Daniels
Oz, Nancy Eimers
Working in Flour, Jeff Friedman
Scorpio Rising: Selected Poems, Richard Katrovas
The Politics, Benjamin Paloff
Copperhead, Rachel Richardson

2012
Now Make an Altar, Amy Beeder
Still Some Cake, James Cummins
Comet Scar, James Harms
Early Creatures, Native Gods, K. A. Hays
That Was Oasis, Michael McFee
Blue Rust, Joseph Millar
Spitshine, Anne Marie Rooney
Civil Twilight, Margot Schilpp

2013
Oregon, Henry Carlile
Selvage, Donna Johnson
At the Autopsy of Vaslav Nijinsky, Bridget Lowe
Silvertone, Dzvinia Orlowsky
Fibonacci Batman: New & Selected Poems (1991–2011), Maureen Seaton
When We Were Cherished, Eve Shelnutt
The Fortunate Era, Arthur Smith
Birds of the Air, David Yezzi

2014
Night Bus to the Afterlife, Peter Cooley
Alexandria, Jasmine Bailey
Dear Gravity, Gregory Djanikian
Pretenders, Jeff Friedman
How I Went Red, Maggie Glover
All That Might Be Done, Samuel Green
Man, Ricardo Pau-Llosa
The Wingless, Cecilia Llompart

2015
The Octopus Game, Nicky Beer
The Voices, Michael Dennis Browne
Domestic Garden, John Hoppenthaler
We Mammals in Hospitable Times, Jynne Dilling Martin
And His Orchestra, Benjamin Paloff
Know Thyself, Joyce Peseroff
cadabra, Dan Rosenberg
The Long Haul, Vern Rutsala
Bartram's Garden, Eleanor Stanford

2016
Something Sinister, Hayan Charara
The Spokes of Venus, Rebecca Morgan Frank
Adult Swim, Heather Hartley
Swastika into Lotus, Richard Katrovas
The Nomenclature of Small Things, Lynn Pedersen
Hundred-Year Wave, Rachel Richardson
Where Are We in This Story, Sarah Rosenblatt
Inside Job, John Skoyles
Suddenly It's Evening: Selected Poems, John Skoyles

2017
Disappeared, Jasmine V. Bailey
Custody of the Eyes, Kimberly Burwick
Dream of the Gone-From City, Barbara Edelman
Sometimes We're All Living in a Foreign Country, Rebecca Morgan Frank
Rowing with Wings, James Harms
Windthrow, K. A. Hays
We Were Once Here, Michael McFee
Kingdom, Joseph Millar
The Histories, Jason Whitmarsh

2018
World Without Finishing, Peter Cooley
May Is an Island, Jonathan Johnson
The End of Spectacle, Virginia Konchan
Big Windows, Lauren Moseley
Bad Harvest, Dzvinia Orlowsky

The Turning, Ricardo Pau-Llosa
Immortal Village, Kathryn Rhett
No Beautiful, Anne Marie Rooney
Last City, Brian Sneeden
Imaginal Marriage, Eleanor Stanford
Black Sea, David Yezzi

2019
Brightword, Kimberly Burwick
The Complaints, W. S. Di Piero
Ordinary Chaos, Kimberly Kruge
Blue Flame, Emily Pettit
Afterswarm, Margot Schilpp

2020
Build Me a Boat, Michael Dennis Browne
Sojourners of the In-Between, Gregory Djanikian
The Marksman, Jeff Friedman
Disturbing the Light, Samuel Green
Any God Will Do, Virginia Konchan
My Second Work, Bridget Lowe
Flourish, Dora Malech
Petition, Joyce Peseroff
Take Nothing, Deborah Pope

2021
The One Certain Thing, Peter Cooley
The Knives We Need, Nava EtShalom
Oh You Robot Saints!, Rebecca Morgan Frank
Dark Harvest: New & Selected Poems, 2001–2020, Joseph Millar
Glorious Veils of Diane, Rainie Oet
Yes and No, John Skoyles